Ice Cream Man

Dax Flame

Ice Cream Man

I work at an ice cream shop in Los Angeles.

I used to be extremely famous on YouTube—16th most subscribed of all time. It was 2007 and I was 15. A few years later I was cast in a Warner Brothers movie called Project X, and a year after that I acted in 21 Jump Street. I was paid $40,000 for each role. But somewhere along the way something went wrong, my career dried up, and now I'm 27 and working as an ice cream man.

I like beautiful weather, drinking smoothies, days off, laughing, finishing exercising, and watching movies.

I want a promotion at work, more free time, a new wardrobe, a new girlfriend, and eventually a movie career again.

Peppermint Pattie

The other day a balding man in glasses, a Hawaiian shirt, and nice slacks came into the ice cream shop with his wife. He seemed like quite a modest person, but he also liked to make jokes, like when I asked him if they were up to anything exciting that evening, he said, "*This* is exciting. Ice cream's the highlight." I politely pretended to laugh, because lots of people make that joke. He seemed very friendly, but also very boring to be honest, but not in a bad way, just in the way older people sometimes are.

So he told me what he wanted, I scooped his cone of peppermint ice cream, and as I turned to take his wife's order I heard him let out a shout of terror— not surprise, but *terror*.

I turned my head just in time to see him catch his falling ice cream, which had fallen from its cone down his shirt and into his hand. I was surprised that's what the shout had been about, because it seemed like such a horrified shout.

His wife looked surprised, and the man, ice cream dripping down his blushing cheeks and chin, had a hard time making eye contact with me as I asked if he'd like me to replace the ice cream. He said it was

2

fine since he caught it before it touched the ground or anything, and began pushing it back onto the cone. I tried to act like I hadn't noticed too much by turning to his wife and asking her order. I gave her some ice cream, rang them up, and they went on their way.

Shortly after they left I replayed the scene in my mind and began judging the man, thinking, "I would never scream in horror about ice cream falling from its cone. I'd scream in horror if someone was driving towards me on the road and I realized they weren't gonna stop and they're going to crush me. I wouldn't scream about ice cream. The oldest saying in the book is 'Don't cry over spilled milk.' Worst case scenario your shirt gets ruined, which isn't a big deal. And if the ice cream hits the ground I'll replace it free of charge."

But then I made myself realize that people are just doing their best, and you can't judge them. Maybe he had parents that yelled at him for spilling things when he was little, and now that's one of his biggest challenges. Or maybe the shirt he was wearing was a very special gift from his wife, or a dead relative. You never know what past a person has or what's in their head.

Sex

I've only had sex once since my ex-girlfriend and I broke up.

I met the girl through Tinder. My friends had created an account for me a couple weeks before, and she was my first date. Talking to each other on the app had been fun, and when we met at a bar I couldn't believe how gorgeous she was. We immediately clicked, and within ten minutes we were holding hands as we walked through the crowd, her hand soft and lovely. And within thirty or so minutes we were kissing by the dance floor. It was like a movie. It was so special. The only strange thing was that while we were in the middle of a conversation she would occasionally just say, "Hello." She did it about four times, and I didn't know how to feel about it.

She suggested we hang out at my apartment instead of the bar, and in the Uber we kissed a lot. It was very different from my ex-girlfriend. My ex-girlfriend and I hadn't kissed until the sixth date. But I thought that maybe this was a different version of how love could work.

At my apartment she asked if she could borrow one of my shirts, because she wanted to put it on and take off all the rest of her clothes. I handed her a shirt and she went into the bathroom and then came out in just the shirt and sat on my bed. We began to kiss and then we had sex. It was very very fun.

Afterwards though, she became a little strange. She put her hand on my neck and squeezed it and said she wanted me to be hers and no one else's. I said I wanted the same thing. She squeezed harder, choking me a little, and I didn't know what to say, and then she stopped. She did a few more things that seemed kind of weird, but I can't explain it really.

I dropped her off at her apartment the next day. There were weird things I didn't understand, but mostly I was just incredibly excited. It made me think a lot about my ex, but also made me think there was a new future for me.

The girl texted me a few times that day and it was fun. Then she texted me a few times in the middle of the night and when I didn't respond until the next day she was kind of mad at me. But she forgave me after I explained I had been sleeping, though I had to apologize twice before she said she accepted the apology.

We made plans to have dinner at her apartment a couple days later, and that's when I felt the most strange. She was holding a knife cutting up some bell peppers she was gonna cook, and I suddenly started feeling very paranoid. I told her I needed to step into the hallway to make a phone call and she pleaded with me to just call them from right there in her kitchen, but after a minute of telling her I wouldn't be able to focus unless I was alone in the hallway she relented. I went and stood in the hallway, took a couple breaths, and then without even thinking I was speed-walking down the hall to the elevator, and then I was in my car driving home.

The next day and a couple times over the next few months I tried to text her but she never texted back.

That's the only time I've had sex since my ex, and we broke up two years ago. (We'd dated for almost a year before breaking up. She's the only girlfriend I've ever had. Besides her and the girl from Tinder I've only ever kissed one other girl—a girl I met on a road trip when I was 23. We'd met at a hostel and she traveled along my road trip with me. I've only kissed those three girls.)

Senior Scooper

I've been working at the shop for nine months now. We got a new general manager three months ago. In the past month I've asked him for a raise twice. I've also asked him for a promotion to shift manager twice. The last time I asked he told me not to ask any more until the end of summer, but that we'd discuss some new position at the performance review the following week.

At the review he told me about a position called senior scooper. It's one step up from scooper, one step below shift manager. It gets paid one extra dollar an hour, and there is the added responsibility of having to train new employees and be more on top of things. I want the gig now, but he says I'll have to wait until the end of summer so I can prove to him that I can do tasks without being asked. He says I need to fill the pint freezer and taster spoons without being asked, and that I need to make waffle cones without being asked as well.

I feel like he's missing the point though. Those three tasks aren't the only ways I can offer value. I already do these things, and I offer value in so many other ways, and just because he's new he feels like I need to prove it to him, despite the fact that I've been here for nine months.

So yeah, frustrating to have another opportunity dangled in front of me, but he does at least sound like he means it when he says I can have the promotion by the end of summer. But by then I'd also like to get a movie role.

Money

I get paid $15 per hour at the ice cream shop. You may think that's a lot, but the rent for my studio apartment is $1,300 per month.

I could go on Craigslist and find a place to move with roommates, but I've lived in this neighborhood the whole time I've lived in Los Angeles and feel very connected to it. I do not want to lose it.

(Despite money being tight, I try to always keep a cushion of about $300 in my bank account that I don't use, just in case anything goes wrong.)

Cleaning

Today the Deep Clean List included cleaning both bathrooms. I told Mason that I'd clean one if he cleaned the other. He replied, "If you're gonna do the job you might as well finish the job." I didn't know what he meant, and he clarified that I should clean both bathrooms. I said it would be more fair if we each did one. He replied, "When I start a job I just finish it. I don't do it halfway." I asked if he wanted to clean both bathrooms. He said yes. So I ended up not having to clean the bathrooms at all today.

(Mason is a 43-year-old man from Alabama, and is an entry-level scooper like me. He has a very high energy level, is very kind to children, and drinks at least two Cokes per shift.)

Hair

My hair is long and curly now. I haven't cut it in ten months. It's not a coincidence that I haven't cut my hair the whole time I've been at the job. I told myself I wouldn't get it cut until I either got a promotion, a raise, or booked a movie gig. I hate having long hair, so I've been using it as motivation to succeed.

It wasn't an easy decision to come to. Previously in life I've gotten a haircut about every six or seven weeks. But shortly after I started the job my friend Kelly asked if I'd be in her short film, and after I said yes she said I should grow my hair out for it. The shoot would end in January, meaning I'd have to walk around with shaggy hair much longer than I'd like, but I thought the short would open some doors in entertainment so I said sure.

We shot the first day of the shoot in mid-December. It went well. It was very fun to be back in front of a camera. The last two days were to be shot a few weeks later.

A week before we were supposed to film those final two days I woke up in a wild mood, sort of over-whelmed with life, and couldn't get myself out of bed, not until I decided to make an appointment at a nearby barbershop. I texted Kelly letting her know I was on my way to get a haircut. She replied asking me not to do it, saying if I got a haircut the short wouldn't make sense, as the whole short was supposed to take place over the course of one day. Since I was in a wild mood and kind of freaking out a little bit I texted her a lie:

Unfortunately my grandpa passed away this year and it is something we do in my family where every Christmas the oldest man in the family gives a hair-cut to all the other men in the family, and normally I might be able to say "I'm gonna sit it out this year" but since my grandpa died this'll be my dad's first time to be the oldest man in the family and so it will be very special for him, and I don't want to sit it out. I wish we could but can we just do it like this?

She called me right away to ask what was going on, and I asked her to write a haircut line into the short for my character, but she said that'd be complicated and unnecessary, and told me that since we'd filmed out of order there'd be no way of making it work anyways. I was gonna ask if maybe I could wear a hat in whatever scenes were out of order, but then I took a deep breath and, not wanting to blow my first acting opportunity I'd had in a while, decided to stop pushing it and instead apologized for making things complicated and told her I wouldn't be cutting it.

So I was forced to wait another week, and it was during that week that I made the decision about not getting it cut until I accomplished one of those goals. I told myself, "You know what... I'm going to use this hair as motivation. It will weigh me down until I am able to burst through and succeed in some form—movies ideally, but a promotion at work, too."

And the final two days of the shoot went very well.

Free Ice Cream

Every day we're allowed to have one free cup of ice cream. I do not eat ice cream, so instead I'll usually just take a bottle of sparkling water. One day though, I was talking to this very sweet woman and when it was time for her to pay I told her she could have my free ice cream for the day. She was very grateful and it was a very sweet moment. I asked if I could take a photo with her and for a few weeks that was my phone background. I've given ice cream to 10 or 15 people since, and have pictures with most of them.

Travel

I used to travel everywhere.

I didn't know how to fill my days and I was quite rich, so I travelled around, stayed in hostels, wrote movie ideas, talked to strangers, wrote a book, and looked for love.

I went to India, Mexico, Europe, Peru, Thailand, all over the US, and even Russia. Always solo.

My trip to Russia happened because a 23-year-old magazine editor in Moscow heard about the book I wrote about my travels, interviewed me about it over Skype, and then asked if I'd come read from it at an event they were having for their magazine.

I was already living in LA at the time, and had just met the girl who would eventually become my first girlfriend/first love/first heartbreak. But at the time I was just obsessed with her, and we weren't together yet, and I didn't know how to woo her.

So I accepted the editor's invitation, and she flew me out, in the dead of Russian winter, and I walked around the city with her for a day, jet-lagged but excited, and at night we sat in my hotel room and played truth or dare, and dared each other to sing songs and do dances, and truthed each other into telling our deepest secrets, and we immediately became extremely close friends, especially because she let me ask her endless advice about how to woo the girl who would eventually become my first love/first ex. And then the next night I read from my book and a translator translated, and the crowd seemed to like it I guess, but I don't know if they really did, and then they showed some clips of my vlogs and my movie scenes, and they were kind of quiet the whole time, and afterward I went out to some bars with the editor and her husband and friends and it was a very fun time, then I flew back to LA and tried to put all the editor's love advice to use, and a few months later I had a girlfriend for the first time.

Shift Manager

Yesterday before the assistant manager came in to close I scrubbed the stainless steel counters behind the dipping cabinet until they were flawless. On top of that, I grabbed the stainless steel polish spray and rubbed them down with that.

When the assistant manager came in, I pointed the polished counters out to her and asked her to mention it to the new GM. I also mentioned that I'd switched out four tubs and pinted what was left over. She said she would mention it, and I believe her because she's actually very cool and supportive, but I also don't trust her to explain it fully. I e-mailed the new GM this morning. I told him to watch the security tapes from yesterday to see how I'd worked. I've e-mailed him saying to watch the footage two other times besides yesterday and he does it and says good work but he still doesn't say anything about a raise or promotion.

I sometimes feel like the only way they'd realize the value I offer is if I quit, because then they'd see what they'd lost.

Toby

I wrote a script called *Toby* around the time of my breakup. A month ago I re-wrote some of it and showed it to my agent. He liked it but said it probably wouldn't get funded. He thinks I should write a TV show. I had one gameshow idea but he said it should be a narrative pilot. I don't have any narrative pilot ideas. And plus, I wrote *Toby* specifically hoping it'd be appealing to a large market. It has violence and romance and heartbreak and high stakes and everything a big-budget movie needs.

Famous

Many people recognize me scooping ice cream. Usually they ask if I was in 21 Jump Street, though some of them know my YouTube videos. One or two times the person has been super excited, and one time this guy made me uncomfortable by trying to sneak some photos of me.

One interesting thing that happened was that I scooped this man some ice cream, and as I rang him up he asked where he knew me from, and I said I used to do some acting, and he asked if I was in 21 Jump Street, and when I said yes he said oh my gosh, and told me he was an animator on some unreleased Will Smith animated movie, and that they used my performance in 21 Jump Street as the main inspiration for a character voiced by Tom Holland in the movie. He said my character in 21 Jump Street was pretty much him in high school, and that he and the animators kept watching clips of the performance for reference to base the animated character on. When I got home I looked the movie up and saw that it's called *Spies in Disguise* and comes out around Christmas. I'll definitely go see it.

Vision

On a slow day a couple weeks ago I rearranged the tables in the eating area so that all four of them were connected together, forming one big communal table. I did this in order to make a more communal experience for people—so that strangers would meet and talk and form connections. I have specifically heard the owners of the company talk about how they want their stores to be a gathering place for the community. But when I showed the new GM how I arranged the tables he faked being impressed and asked me to put it back, giving some nonsense reason why they should be that way, but really just wanting things to be his way instead of mine.

I also sometimes play slower more relaxing instrumental music in the store in order to offset the sugar high the little kids experience, to try to balance them out a bit. I don't want them getting so amped up by sugar and thumping music that they drive away with a headache, crying & feeling unbalanced. Each of the last two times the GM has walked in while that's been playing though, he's asked me to change it to something more "upbeat", or just changed it himself to early 2000's hits.

I'd like to see the store move in a much different direction than the one he's taking it in.

Ex

My ex makes vlogs and for a while I watched them. I'd see her going to movie premieres, getting brand deals, traveling the world, etc. Eventually I realized I shouldn't watch them anymore, so I stopped.

The reason we broke up is she wanted to know herself better and felt like she should be single while she explored some things. She also said maybe we'd be friends someday, but that we should take a three month break from talking after the breakup in order to get over each other. I tried texting her a few different times before those three months were up, but this kind of pushed her further away and eventually it just turned into a forever break from talking and we haven't spoken since.

But I tell you what, when you're in love it's really something special. I don't regret anything, because I got to experience something really special. And I know she loved me for a bit, too. So I have no complaints. None at all.

The Owners

The company I work for is owned by a husband and wife in their 40's. They seem like very kind people. They started the company in Chicago, where they have 10 or so locations, and they recently decided they'd like to start expanding all across the globe (starting with our LA store). Although I'm not personally a fan of ice cream I do like what they have to say about their vision for things. They talk about wanting to create an experience at their stores that brings people together, reminiscent of the soda shops of the 1950's. I like that.

I've met them both very briefly, but honestly was a little nervous to talk to them, as it was right after I'd first started the job and didn't want to do anything wrong.

In the time I've worked for the company they've sent out three different e-mails to the entire staff. One of them was at Christmas to tell us thank you, and that they'd be giving us each a $50 Christmas bonus on our next check. I thought this was very nice (even if it wasn't a ton, they didn't have to do that) and sent a brief reply saying I worked in the LA store and thanks for the bonus.

The next two e-mails (also sent to the entire staff) were sent on consecutive days a couple months later saying that they found out someone in the company had been stealing and had to be let go. And the next e-mail said that it was difficult to be expanding and that they were sad they couldn't make it feel as Mom & Pop as it used to feel when they had less stores, but that they were going to try to maintain that Mom & Pop energy. I didn't really know what to say so I just said that sounded tough and I appreciated the opportunity to work for them.

Besides that, the only other time I've communicated directly with them was a few months ago when I was just getting over the flu, right before I released my documentary, and I drew a picture of the two of them from an image I found on Google. I liked the drawing enough, so I scanned it and e-mailed it over to them, and they replied thanks for sending it and that they loved it. It legit took me an hour or two to draw, so I was happy they had the courtesy to thank me.

Lately I've been thinking of e-mailing them again. And I've also been thinking of bringing in the drawing of the owners and asking the new GM if they'd be interested in displaying it. It's not great or anything (drawing definitely isn't my main talent), but it might add a sweet, personal touch.

Karma/Past Lives

I have a friend who focuses a lot on spirituality, and a few months ago she explained some stuff about karma to me. Essentially she told me that karma is a universal law that carries over from all your actions, including in past lives (she was talking about reincarnation). She was saying that potentially some of the stuff I've been going through could be due to negative actions from previous lives of mine, and that there's a message in it for me to decipher to move on to good karma. I thought it kind of made sense, but I haven't seen her since then in order to pick her brain more and get her to clarify what exactly I can do about it. So nowadays that's always in the back of my head, but I don't know what to do about it.

I would imagine I need to do some good deeds, which I always try to do anyways. But I'm also left wondering what I did wrong previously. I guess it wasn't even ME who did it. Some other person whose karma and soul got passed into me, but then I was born with an original brain, uninfluenced by those past lives, just ready and new, with karma in the background.

Sandwich Board

A sandwich board is one of those foldable chalk boards businesses put outside their shop with messages like "*Ice Cream Inside!*" in order to get people to come in.

Our sandwich board was inside a few days ago, completely blank, so I drew a picture of the owners on one side, wrote "*Mom & Pop Style Experience*" on the other side, and then displayed it out on the sidewalk.

It took like half an hour and I did it when the shift manager was on lunch break since it was a slow day and I was bored.

When I came into work the next day I saw that the drawing had been erased and replaced. Inside the store no one said anything about it to me. I could tell from the handwriting that the person who'd done it was the assistant manager. The fact that she did it behind my back kind of irked me. But since she's such a nice person I didn't want to just keep it in and resent her for it, so I took the sign inside, erased her drawing, and I was about to redraw the owners but then I realized that would be passive aggressive and I should just talk to her about it so I walked upstairs to the office and said, "The sandwich board is blank. What should I draw on it?" She asked why it was blank and I hesitated for a moment before telling her the truth that I'd erased it. She didn't ask why, she just said sorry she'd erased my drawing and asked if I could rewrite what she'd written on the board because she wanted to promote the new sundae. I said yes and also apologized for erasing her drawing and I felt kind of embarrassed but also felt good that the air had been cleared.

Indoor Garden

A couple years ago, just before I was about to be dead-broke for the first time in my life, I had an idea for an invention. It was a garden that would grow indoors with artificial UV light, and it'd automatically water itself, and would be linked up to an app on your phone. It was a great idea, and I figured if I could pull it off I could get pretty rich, and could avoid ever having to get a real job.

So I set out to make it, and I knew the first step would be to procure a small initial investment for patents and prototypes and whatnot, which I could then show to bigger investors in meetings. I felt the best place to find the initial investment was on the internet, so I created a Kickstarter, promising backers a documentary about the invention process if they invested.

The Kickstarter was successfully funded, so I then had about a month to create 3D models, develop a business plan, set up meetings, and procure my next investment. I filmed the whole process, but at the end of the month I realized the money wasn't gonna come in time and that I'd have to get a real job instead, so I set the invention aside while I began driving Lyft and doing a food delivery job, and I never ended up pursuing the invention again.

I did however edit the footage I'd filmed into a documentary, and after about ten months of driving jobs I got the ice cream job, and then I began submitting the documentary to film festivals, and in the back of my mind I hoped it would get accepted and save me from the ice cream job by opening up entertainment doors. But every festival I submitted it to rejected it, and so I posted it on YouTube, and it's yet to open any entertainment doors, but I think it still will someday. It's definitely a good part of my creative portfolio now.

Sabatoge

A couple weeks ago I decided, "I'm done. Bullshit."

Nothing specific happened—nothing outside of the stuff I've already mentioned—such as the new GM not noticing or acknowledging my efforts—I just suddenly realized, "I'm done. I need to find something new."

I printed up 30 resumes the next day and walked around the neighborhood handing out almost every one of them. Then I got on Craigslist and spent a few days e-mailing out another 40 or 50 resumes.

I got one interview out of it. Some food place in Atwater. She seemed to like me but I haven't heard back, so she probably went another direction for the position.

I also got one other potential interview from a donut place in echo park, but then they stopped e-mailing me.

So yeah, I've given up on getting a promotion or raise. I don't care anymore. I'm not gonna go on like this for the whole summer. And yet it doesn't seem any other positions are opening up for me. Yet.

But in the meantime work at the shop has become extremely difficult. Because now I'm no longer working up the ladder. Instead it's turned into a sort of purgatory. And I've started misbehaving. Sabotaging them.

When I enter flavors into the POS/register, I enter the incorrect flavor so they get incorrect data. On top of that I told one of the other scoopers that I overheard he's getting a raise, that way he'll talk to them about it and get mad at them as well. I hid the espresso measurer and they had to buy a new one. Only like $15 probably, which doesn't mean anything to the company in the grand scheme of things, but it still felt good.

I want to find a way to really throw a wrench in the system, though. I don't know what, but maybe like... I don't know... I want to convince everyone to quit at the same time as me. But I know it's not gonna work because everyone has the same problem as me—there's no better jobs available right away. It takes time.

The dream is: I sell a screenplay and I hire all my coworkers to be PA's on it, and I give them all jobs as they quit the ice cream job, and the new GM is fired because the owners of the company realize he's an awful manager who can't manage our morale.

Gameshow

I was trying to take my agent's advice to write a narrative pilot but couldn't come up with any ideas, so then I started trying to adapt a feature screenplay I wrote in 2015 into a pilot. It's a Christmas-themed screenplay about a young investor facing a big obstacle, but I don't really know how to adapt it into TV format so I've just been stuck. *Toby* would probably be an easier screenplay to adapt, but it works better as a feature than a series, so I don't want to ruin it.

What I'd like to do is just cast fate to the wind and spend all $300 of my emergency fund on making a gameshow pilot. The cinematographers who shot my documentary ranged from about $200 to $350 per day of filming, so I could maybe ask one of them to shoot it for $200, and then I could use the other $100 as the cash prize for the winner of the gameshow.

The premise for the gameshow is this: it'd be a smoothie-themed gameshow, and each week I'd find two contestants (perhaps from Craigslist, and then through submissions once the show built up an audience) and they'd compete in various challenges. One of the challenges would be that I'd give each contestant the same ingredients to make a smoothie with, and whoever made the best tasting smoothie would win. And then there'd be time-based challenges as well, and I'd be hosting everything. Whoever wins would get a $100 prize, and the value would go up as the show developed an audience.

If I shot the pilot and it came out well I could try to pitch it to YouTube or some network or something, and if the stars aligned maybe it'd work out. I'm just a little worried about spending all of my emergency funds on the pilot at the moment because I know I'm supposed to renew my ID and license plates in October and it's going to cost about $200. Ideally I'd get a higher paying job so I could fund it without thinking about that. I could also ask someone to film it for free on a phone, but I want it to look high quality so it has a chance of being picked up by some network. At some point though maybe I'll just go for it.

Ice Cream Alley

There are three other ice cream shops within walking distance of my shop. So four ice cream shops total within a one mile radius. Each shop is sort of fancy and expensive. I don't eat ice cream, but people talk highly of all the places, including mine. Our shop is the newest and I've been here since the beginning. I've heard the new general manager and assistant manager talk about how we're friendly neighbors with the other places, not competitive, but I don't believe them.

Hollywood

Back in February, after only a few months at the ice cream shop, I found myself on Hollywood Blvd. down on my knees on the cement in front of the Grauman's Chinese Theatre, my hands placed in the handprints of Robert DeNiro, my eyes closed.

What was I doing?

Waiting.

I was waiting for some inspiration to enter me. I was trying to absorb some kind of energy. I don't know. I don't know what I was doing.

I went around to all the different handprints in the cement, from some of my very favorite actors and entertainers (Jim Carrey, Clint Eastwood, Tim Burton, etc.), bent down to my knees, put my hands in theirs, and waited there with my eyes closed each time, trying to gain something.

What was there to lose?

Down on my knees I'm not sure that anything changed. I tried extremely hard to focus but I didn't know what to focus on, and I'm not sure if I gained or absorbed anything.

A few months later I released my documentary.

Dry Ice

Today a shipment of a specialty flavor of came in from Chicago. It was packed in a brown box filled with dry ice, so I put on some rubber gloves, pulled the ice cream out, put it away, and then the shift manager and I put the dry ice in a bowl, added water, and played with the steam for a while.

After a moment the shift manager went on her lunch break and the new GM came downstairs to ask if the shipment had come in. I told him we'd just put it away and when he saw the dry ice he said, "Oh my god, I love dry ice," and came behind the counter to play around with it and to make small talk.

I stepped away from the bowl so he could play with the steam, and after a couple comments about the things he learned about dry ice working as a bartender in Seattle, I observed that he'd gotten a haircut. He said thanks, and then he tried to compliment me by saying that my long hair worked well for me, and that it frames my face well. But it felt like he was slapping me in the face. It felt like he was saying, "I know why you're growing your hair out. Keep it growing. Your position as scooper suits you."

As soon as he went upstairs I threw the dry ice in the trash.

Crazy Teen

When I lived back home, in middle school, I used to slide notes under the bathroom door when my mom was in there to try to make her think a stranger was in the house. They'd say things like, "We've taken your son"

Days Off

I had Saturday off, which was very nice, and I was supposed to work Sunday and Monday before having Tuesday off, but then I decided to fake being sick and call out Sunday and Monday, so I ended up having four straight days off. With the time off I went to a museum, went to the park, saw a friend, went to a restaurant, went to the gym, went to the grocery store. It was my first time faking sick in my time working at the shop, and it made me feel very good. I had a great time.

Fitness

Once I moved to LA I began going to the gym and prioritizing sleep, and when I started gaining muscle I realized I wasn't the nerd everyone always said I was.

The ice cream job interferes with my sleep a little bit since the store's open late but otherwise my health is almost perfect, which I'm very grateful for, and which I would imagine means I have some good karma built up as well.

Hollywood

Ryan Gosling came into the ice cream shop the day after I released my documentary. I was in a sort of daze that day, as I'd been up very late the previous two nights making sure the upload had rendered and processed correctly. He came in around 6:00pm, just after I'd gotten in to start a closing shift. He was with Eva Mendes and their children. Years before, I'd auditioned to play the lead in his directorial debut, *Lost River*, and had received several callbacks, including a chemistry read with Christina Hendricks, but then the role went to someone else. It was my first time seeing him since then, and he seemed very happy to see me, saying hello, asking how I was, and congratulating me after I told him about the documentary. He told Eva who I was and her eyes became very wide as she had a recollection and said, "I'm a big fan of your work," and, "We used to watch your stuff together all the time." I said thanks and then scooped them some ice cream and rang them up.

The *Lost River* auditions had taken place in 2012, the same year *Project X*, *21 Jump Street*, and *The Watch* were released. I was a hot hot hot piece of

Hollywood property for a moment, and came close to landing starring roles in a few other movies that also didn't pan out. Auditions slowed down for a while after the *Lost River* one, and nowadays I get none at all, but the thing about Hollywood is you should never give up because everything can change in an instant.

Sabatoge pt. 2

I spent 20 minutes organizing everything under the register Monday. It was a mess and I got it extremely neat and organized. No one noticed or acknowledged it, so I doubled down on sabotage mode the rest of the week.

Wednesday I gave away five free ice creams. Throughout the day I would select one kind customer and tell them, "It's on me today". This cost the company at least $25 in sales. If they had given me a raise it would have only cost them $6 that day. (One dollar for each hour—all I've been asking for is a one dollar raise.)

Thursday I gave nothing away free, but Friday and Saturday I gave away 8 free ice creams (at least a $40 value each day).

Charlie Puth

As a teenage YouTube star I received thousands upon thousands of hate comments and messages, but none of them impacted me more negatively than the ones I received from a wannabe YouTuber named Charlie Puth. At the time he had no followers at all, and the only reason his jealousy infused hate messages stuck out was because they attacked something that no one else really focused on as much—my singing and music talent. As a teenager who lacked much self-awareness I felt I was a pretty decent singer despite being almost completely tone-deaf. But I still enjoyed singing, even if I wasn't perfect at it. The messages I received from this person were vicious though, and very discouraging. I eventually forgot about the messages, until years later when I saw the name Charlie Puth on TV. The wannabe YouTuber had become a legitimate major pop star, doing duets with Meghan Trainor, Pitbull, and more. And all of a sudden all of the comments came back to me and filled me with the same sense of discouragement and self-doubt that they had all those years before.

(This is why I think karma is based on past lives rather than your current life, because if it was based on your current life Charlie would be lying face down in a gutter, begging for crumbs.)

Co-workers

My 35-year-old coworker Jackson has a podcast and likes to write screenplays. He told me that when he and his girlfriend return to New York for the holidays he's gonna buy her an engagement ring at some antique store out there. I told him congrats, and asked how he planned to propose. He said maybe he'd put a message in a fortune cookie and then have a romantic dinner at a Chinese place with her, but she doesn't like Chinese food, so he was trying to think of some other option. I said he should propose to her at the ice cream shop so we could all do some stuff to make it special for them. He said he wanted it to be separate from his work-life though, and that made sense to me.

Another one of my co-workers is moving to Kansas next week because there's a guy there she thinks she may be in love with.

It's interesting to see how everyone's life unfolds.

Baby Bat

I worked a closing shift last night and fell asleep around 2:00am but for some reason woke up at 6:00am. This happens sometimes, and luckily today I wasn't that tired when I woke up, so I decided it was a good day to drive across town and visit the forest, as I hadn't been around nature in a little while.

I hiked for about an hour into the forest before deciding it was time to stop. I sat on a rock beside a little stream and watched the water. After a moment or two I saw a little creature to my left, about the size of a credit card, and assumed it was a frog. But after another moment of looking that way I realized it was something else and stood up to get a better view. It soon registered that it was a baby bat.

It was extremely cute, crawling along the ground, and flying/fluttering very short distances. Soon it reached the stream, where it climbed up onto a big rock. I didn't know bats could climb like that. Watching it sit atop the big rock I wondered if it had climbed there just to get into the shade. But when it tried to fly again it only went a couple inches and then plunged into the stream. I thought maybe I'd have to try to save it, but then I saw that it knew how to swim. It swam back to the stream's shore and climbed out. I was amazed to see that bats could swim.

Back on land it crawled across the rocks in the opposite direction of the stream, wet now. I had a feeling that maybe something was wrong with the bat, that maybe it had gotten lost from its herd or had broken a wing. I felt very bad for it, but wasn't sure how to help, and didn't have my phone to look things up. A big lizard approached on a log and appeared to be sizing the bat up. I scared it away. Other than that though I didn't know what to do, so when it crawled up under the log out of my sight I wished it good luck and began walking back.

The craziest thing about it all though is that just before I began my hike, when I was getting out of my car, I'd seen a black truck with a license plate that had a batman reference. It said: DKGOTHM

Health Inspector

After a month of submitting resumes I received one more interview last week. It was to work at a deli. They said they'd call by the end of the weekend, but since they didn't I'm assuming they went with someone else.

A few days ago I opened the shop with a new shift manager they just brought in. After we set all the chairs out and displayed the sandwich board and whatnot, she left to go buy food even though she wasn't on her lunch break, and I continued to clean and restock things and help customers.

When she returned she disappeared into the office to eat and "count change" while I had to continue doing everything behind the counter. While doing everything solo, the health inspector showed up and asked if she could look around. I was there last time the health inspector came, so I knew the drill. Last time one of the most experienced shift managers had been there with me, and together we had hurried to empty and refill the sanitizer basin, scrubbed down all the counters, and made sure there were no unlabeled jars or anything. This time though, I was solo, and I was pissed off, and I was feeling rebellious, and I was in a position to deliver the kiss of death.

What I could have done, is I could have filled the sanitizer basin with ice cream, and put some spoons in the sprinkles containers to hint at cross-contamination practices, and put trash all over the counters... I could've gotten us an F.

But I didn't. I just simply cleaned everything up, helped the customers, and did my best to get us an A+. And it worked. The health inspector said, "Everything is very clean. I have no notes at all."

Back home I sent one more e-mail to the GM. I told him to watch the security footage so he could see how I interacted with the inspector, even while serving a rush of customers. I asked him for a pro-motion or raise one more time, against his wishes for me to wait until the end of summer. I also hint-ed at the fact that the new shift manager spent most of the morning in the office and left me to do all the work, which no other shift manager does.

I haven't gotten an e-mail back from him, and I don't know if I will.

Closing

I close tonight but right now I'm off.

I could go do something, but sometimes I wanna just spend some time alone. That's what I feel like right now. My Saturday morning apartment is sunny, the music is pretty, the AC is a miracle. I love life.

Final Meeting

Having almost reached the end of summer I sent the general manager one last e-mail asking for a raise.

The general manager met with me the next day and denied my request.

At the meeting it became clear to me that he doesn't intend to ever give me a promotion or raise. He made excuses. He said some stuff about budget. He said some stuff about, "That's life." All excuses.

I sent the owners an e-mail and am hoping they'll override the GM.

I also finally received another response to one of the resumes I sent out. A new restaurant nearby wants to interview me Friday for a host or server position.

Curly Haired Ice Cream Man

Curly haired ice cream man
Curly haired ice cream man
Curly haired ice cream man
Curly haired ice cream man
Curly haired ice cream man
Curly haired ice cream man
Curly haired ice cream man
Curly haired ice cream man
Curly haired ice cream man
Curly haired ice cream man
Curly haired ice cream man
Curly haired ice cream man
Curly haired ice cream man
Curly haired ice cream man
Curly haired ice cream man

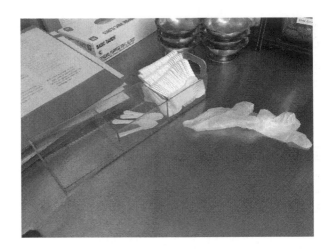

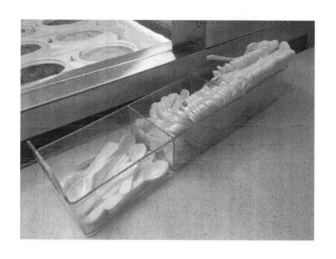

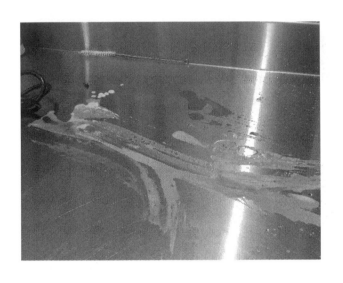

A Wonderful Feeling

Suddenly, out of nowhere, I received an email from my ex. She said she wanted to be friends, and asked if I'd like to meet up. I said yes.

Waiting for her at the park I was quite over-whelmed. And then, after two years of not talking, there she was, walking across the grass, waving hi. We shared a brief hug. We walked around, sat down, talked. We became friends again. It felt very strange but very good.

The next morning I woke up feeling wonderful. At work I felt content. The new GM's presence some-how didn't bother me at all. Nothing felt important anymore, but in a good way. It was like I'd received the answer to a question I didn't know I'd been asking. I don't know what the question was or what the answer is, but that's how it felt.

After work I got in my car and drove to my favorite hiking spot. I hiked for about 15 minutes before reaching a real quiet spot with a great view of the sky. The breeze felt lovely, and the sky was pink and orange with swirls of purple. Sitting there looking at the clouds I had the thought, "*So what if they drop a million atom bombs and blow everything up? So what if an earthquake swallows me and the rest of LA up? The sky is pretty right now and I feel so so good.*"

I sat there another moment, and then I looked up to my right at what I thought was a bird. But it was fluttering around in a sort of weird way, so then I thought maybe it was a big butterfly. But looking at it a moment longer I realized it was a bat. It was the exact size as the bat I'd seen crawling around the forest floor a month earlier. Even though I was on the complete opposite side of town, I had a feeling it was that very bat, or at least I hoped it was, and it felt like it'd come to visit me, to show me that it'd made it, that it'd finally learned to fly.